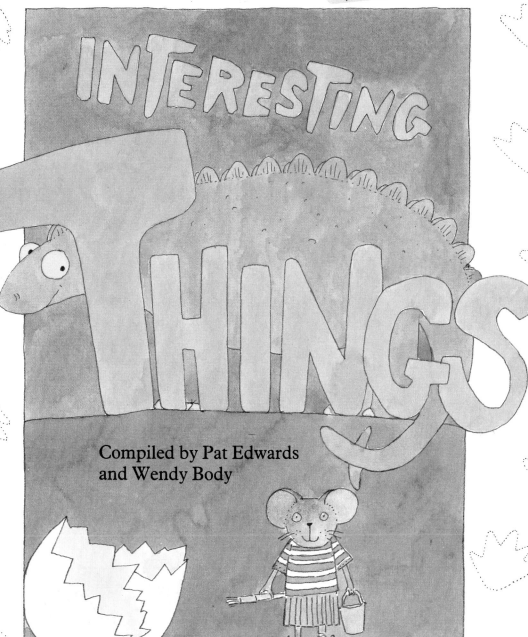

INTERESTING THINGS

Compiled by Pat Edwards
and Wendy Body

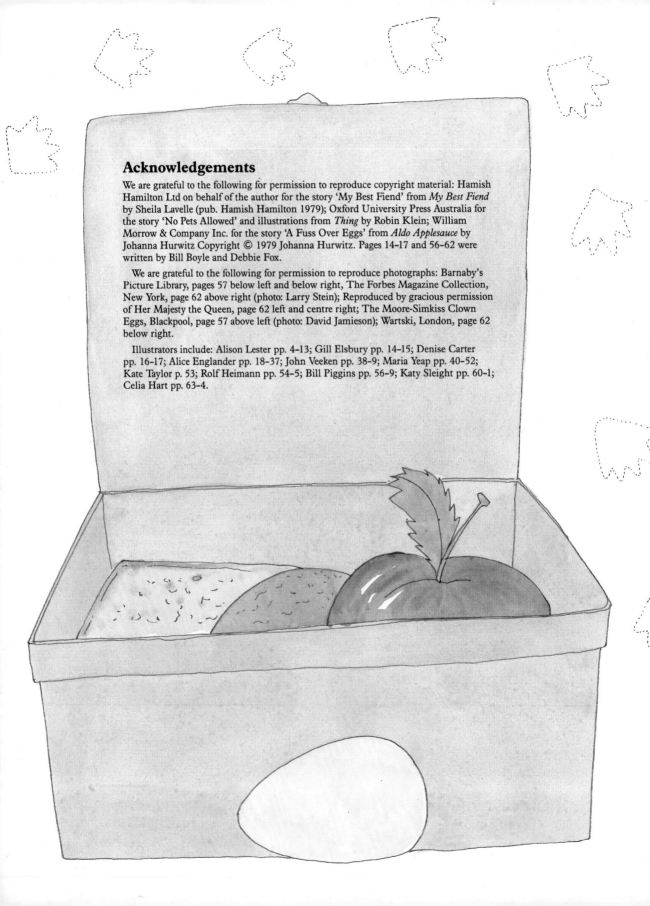

Acknowledgements

We are grateful to the following for permission to reproduce copyright material: Hamish Hamilton Ltd on behalf of the author for the story 'My Best Fiend' from *My Best Fiend* by Sheila Lavelle (pub. Hamish Hamilton 1979); Oxford University Press Australia for the story 'No Pets Allowed' and illustrations from *Thing* by Robin Klein; William Morrow & Company Inc. for the story 'A Fuss Over Eggs' from *Aldo Applesauce* by Johanna Hurwitz Copyright © 1979 Johanna Hurwitz. Pages 14–17 and 56–62 were written by Bill Boyle and Debbie Fox.

We are grateful to the following for permission to reproduce photographs: Barnaby's Picture Library, pages 57 below left and below right, The Forbes Magazine Collection, New York, page 62 above right (photo: Larry Stein); Reproduced by gracious permission of Her Majesty the Queen, page 62 left and centre right; The Moore-Simkiss Clown Eggs, Blackpool, page 57 above left (photo: David Jamieson); Wartski, London, page 62 below right.

Illustrators include: Alison Lester pp. 4–13; Gill Elsbury pp. 14–15; Denise Carter pp. 16–17; Alice Englander pp. 18–37; John Veeken pp. 38–9; Maria Yeap pp. 40–52; Kate Taylor p. 53; Rolf Heimann pp. 54–5; Bill Piggins pp. 56–9; Katy Sleight pp. 60–1; Celia Hart pp. 63–4.

CONTENTS

Fife Council Education Department
King's Road Primary School
King's Crescent, Rosyth KY11 2RS

# NO PETS ALLOWED

Emily Forbes and her mother lived in the top flat and Mrs McIlvray, the owner, lived in the bottom one. Pets weren't allowed in the flats — it was a very strict rule.

One day Emily found a beautiful rock. She picked it up, rubbed it clean with the sleeve of her school jumper and took it home . . .

The rock was a cosy, rounded shape, and a gleaming, rich dark brown, the colour of Marmite in a new jar before anyone shoves a knife in to spread their toast. Emily took it home and put it on the living-room table, propping it up with a lemon squeezer because it was so smooth it tended to roll away.

"Mrs McIlvray couldn't possibly complain about your keeping a rock for a pet," said Emily's mother. "What are you going to call it?"

"I'll call it Thing," said Emily. "It's nice and short and easy to remember." She patted the rock goodnight and went to bed.

Mrs Forbes, who was inclined to be vague about such matters, forgot to turn off the oil heater, and when they got up in the morning the living-room was like a sauna.

"Oh blah!" said Emily. "The heat cracked Thing."

"Rocks don't crack as easily as that," said her mother. "Let me look." She picked it up and found that there *was* a crack, like an opening zip-fastener, and while she was looking it zipped open even more. The rock quivered in her hands, and made a peculiar slithery noise. Mrs Forbes made a louder one, and dropped it nervously on to the carpet.

**E**mily was more curious than alarmed, and she poked at the rock with the point of an HB pencil. Something inside tapped back, so she helpfully tugged the two sections of the rock shell apart. A creature wriggled out, uncoiled itself and blinked at them. It was about half a metre long and a most attractive shade of green, like a Granny Smith apple.

"What on earth can it be?" asked Emily's mother. "I never saw anything like it before!"

"We did a project on dinosaurs at school," said Emily. "I think this could be a baby stegosaurus. They weren't as awful as those dinosaurs they have in horror movies, though. I think they were vegetarians."

"Oh," said Mrs Forbes, relieved. "You can give it that left-over coleslaw in the fridge, then."

"Come along, Thing," said Emily, and the little stegosaurus followed her into the kitchen. He ate the coleslaw, and four ripe bananas Mrs Forbes was saving to use for banana custard, and half a carton of mango yoghurt. While he was eating, he thumped his tail enthusiastically on the floor.

"If you keep him, you must tie newspapers round his tail to muffle the noise," said Mrs Forbes. "It's going to be difficult hiding him from Mrs McIlvray. I think they grow to quite a large size, Emily. Still, I suppose you can deal with each problem as it comes up."

7

he first problem for Emily was the worry about Thing being left on his own while she was at school and her mother was at work. Luckily she discovered that he liked television. While she was having her breakfast, she had the set switched on. Thing looked at it with great interest, then he jumped up on the couch and kneaded his little claws in and out of the couch cushions, making a contented purring noise. So Emily left the set turned on, with the sound very low.

When she came home from school, Thing was still on the couch, watching TV. He seemed to have grown a little during the day. Emily fed him a bunch of silverbeet which she had bought at the greengrocer's on the way home.

rs Forbes phoned from where she worked, as she did every day to make sure Emily got home safely.

"That stegosaurus should really be getting some outdoor exercise," she said. "I don't think dinosaurs just sat around watching TV in prehistoric times. You'll have to smuggle him out into the park, but don't let Mrs McIlvray see you both. And make sure no one notices you in the park, either, Emily. People can be very mean about animals being a nuisance. They're quite likely to whisk Thing off to a museum and put him in a glass box with a label."

Thing seemed to understand the need for quiet, even though he was so young. He padded softly after Emily down the stairs, and curled up his tail so that it wouldn't bump from one step to the next.

9

There weren't any people in the park, and Thing loved it there. He munched weeds and chased after autumn leaves, and rolled over for Emily to tickle his tummy. Then he sat down in the park fountain and gargled.

The only dangerous time was when a young man in a track suit went by, jogging. He blinked and slowed down. "Freeze, Thing!" whispered Emily, and Thing froze to look just the same as the rocks in the fountain, only mossier, so the young man jogged on.

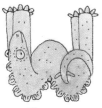hen it was time to go back to the flat, Thing followed Emily obediently, and she got him upstairs without being seen. But soon there was a knock on the door, and Mrs McIlvray stood outside, looking indignant.

"You've gone and brought a Saint Bernard dog in off the street!" she said. "The rule here, young lady, is NO PETS!"

"We don't have a Saint Bernard dog," Emily said truthfully.

"There are large muddy footprints on the steps, and they lead right up to this door!"

"Oh, they must be from my new plastic flippers," Emily said, not so truthfully. "I was testing them out in the park fountain. I'm sorry, and I'll wipe up the marks straight away."

"Kindly don't let it happen again," said Mrs McIlvray.

Emily didn't. She always took two pairs of old woollen socks and put them on Thing before she sneaked him back up the stairs after his daily ten minutes in the park.

Thing was really very little trouble. He spent all day watching television, with the tip of his tail in his mouth at the exciting bits. He didn't seem to mind what programmes were on. He liked them all: cartoons, classical music concerts, the news and weather forecasts, and even talks on gardening and cookery demonstrations.

At night he slept in a soft bed Emily made from a rubber inner tyre tube she got from the corner garage, and an old duffel coat she didn't wear anymore. Thing didn't care that it wasn't a nice, soggy, prehistoric marsh. He circled once or twice, then settled down cosily with his nose resting on the tip of his tail.

He had a double row of bony plates down his back, and Emily kept them beautifully polished with Brasso. He grew to about the size of a small rhinoceros, and then stopped growing. Emily's mother was very relieved.

Robin Klein
illustrated by *Alison Lester*

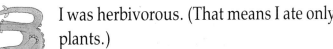
Fully grown, I was about 7 metres long. Would I fit in your bedroom?

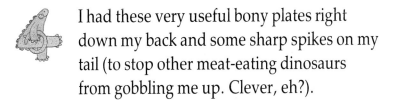
I was found all over the world.

I was herbivorous. (That means I ate only plants.)

I had these very useful bony plates right down my back and some sharp spikes on my tail (to stop other meat-eating dinosaurs from gobbling me up. Clever, eh?).

Scientists say I wasn't very bright, because my brain was only the size of a walnut. But how do they know? None of them was around when I was alive!

13

Eggs

There are two types of egg:
The first kind doesn't contain much food, so the young must hatch out quickly. These young are called larvae and do not look like their parents. They need their parents to help them survive at first.

The frog lays many eggs, which are covered in a protective jelly known as **frogspawn**. The eggs hatch out into tadpoles.

The female cabbage white butterfly lays its eggs on the bottom of a leaf.

The second kind of egg contains a lot of food, so that when the young breaks out of its shell, it is a tiny copy of its parents and can soon look after itself.

Birds' eggs are **incubated** (kept warm) by the female for a few weeks. From time to time the mother bird turns the eggs over. The eggs then hatch. The baby bird is strong enough to peck its way out of the shell.

Some snakes lay their eggs in dead leaves on the ground; the warm sun and soil causes them to hatch. Other snakes give birth to live young (baby snakes). Baby snakes are able to look after themselves from the beginning of their lives.

When the eggs of the stickleback hatch in the nest at the bottom of the pond, the male guards the young for ten days so that they can learn to look after themselves.

The python is one of the few snakes that incubates its eggs. The female python coils its body around a pile of eggs and only leaves them to go for a drink.

The ladybird lays its eggs on a plant covered with tiny insects called **aphids,** on which the baby ladybirds feed.

The turtle comes ashore to lay its eggs in sand. The female turtle digs a pit and lays more than a hundred eggs. She covers the nest of eggs with sand to protect them. The young turtles hatch out by the heat of the sun and they make straight for the sea.

15

Did you know that...?

In October 1961 some examples of the largest known dinosaur eggs were found in southern France. They were 30 centimetres long and over 65 million years old.

The ocean sunfish may produce up to 300 million eggs. Each egg is 1.3 millimetres long. The baby sunfish is about 12.7 millimetres long.

A chicken's egg produced on a poultry farm in America in July 1971 is said to have had a record number of nine yolks.

In test at the University of Missouri in America in 1979, a white leghorn chicken hen laid 371 eggs in 364 days.

The smallest bird's egg was laid by the Vervain hummingbird in Jamaica. It measured less than 10 millimetres in length.

The albatross lays one large egg in a nest of mud and plants. It is incubated by both parents for 65 to 81 days, depending on how large the type of albatross is.

The largest egg produced by any living bird comes from the ostrich. The average egg measures 15–20 centimetres. To boil it you'll need 40 minutes!

My Best Fiend

Playing tricks on people is Angela's favourite hobby. She even does it to me sometimes, and I'm supposed to be her best friend. Once she rushed into our house shouting "Charlie! Quick! Come and see! There's a man walking down the street with no trousers on!" I went dashing out to have a look, but it was only Mr MacLennon in his kilt, and Angela fell about laughing when she saw my face. My dad thought it was funny too, but my mum said Angela was a very rude girl.

Angela does things like that all the time, so it's not really surprising that I thought her laryngitis was just another one of her jokes. It was a Monday morning, and when she called for me on the way to school she had her neck all muffled up in a woolly scarf. I asked her what was the matter, but she could only talk in a hoarse sort of whisper and she told me she'd lost her voice.

Well, I looked at her and all I did was laugh. I was certain it was a trick, especially after what had happened on Friday, so I'd better tell you about that first.

That Friday had been a bad day for Angela, because she was in one of her talkative moods and you know how that always gets on teachers' nerves. My dad says that when Angela is in one of her talkative moods she's even worse than her mother. Anyway, Miss Bennett had to keep on telling her to shut up all day long, and by the last lesson, which was Nature Study, everybody was getting a bit fed up.

We were doing the Life History of the Frog, and the trouble was that Angela knew it all already. In fact the whole class knew it all already because we'd done the Life History of the Frog last year in Mrs Moody's class and the year before in Miss Whiteman's *and* the year before that in Miss Spender's, and it seems to me that you have to do the Life History of the Frog in every class in every school from the kindergarten to the sixth form. Teachers get ever so flustered and upset if you say you've done it before so you have to let them get on with it and pretend it's all new and interesting. But I don't mind doing it all over again because I like drawing those funny little tadpoles with their wiggly tails and I'm getting quite good at them now.

Anyway, Miss Bennett had some baby tadpoles in a jar and she was holding them up in front of the class while she talked so that we could all see them.

"And then, after the eggs hatch out," she said, "the tadpoles feed on the jelly around them." Angela bobbed up out of her chair.

"Please, Miss Bennett," she said. "I saw this programme on the telly the other day. And the man said they don't think that's true any more. Everybody used to think so, but now they've found out that the jelly is only a sort of protection, and the baby tadpoles feed on pondweed and possibly small organisations in the water."

Miss Bennett sighed. "I think you mean organisms, Angela," she said. Angela nodded and sat down.

"Well, that's most interesting," continued Miss Bennett. "You can see how science is discovering new facts all the time. Now, where was I? Oh, yes. The young tadpoles breathe under water by means of —"

"Gills," said Angela, bouncing out of her desk again. "They're very interesting things, Miss Bennett, because they can absorb oxygen from the water."

Miss Bennett frowned. "That's quite correct, Angela," she said. "I'm glad you know so much about it. But I'd rather you didn't interrupt the lesson. There'll be plenty of time for discussion afterwards." Miss Bennett looked down at the jar of tadpoles.

"Now, the hind legs develop first, and then the —" But Angela was on her feet again.

"I'm sorry, Miss Bennett," she said. "But the man on the telly said that all the legs develop at the same time. It only looks as if the hind legs develop first, because the front ones are hidden by the gill flaps."

"Angela!" said Miss Bennett crossly. "I have asked you not to interrupt. If it happens again I shall have to send you out of the room. I don't know what's the matter with you today." Miss Bennett started to walk around the room, stopping at each desk to show us the tadpoles in the jar.

"This is the stage these tadpoles are at now," she went on. "They are growing very rapidly and need lots of food. We can even give them small pieces of meat to nibble and —"

"Excuse me, Miss Bennett," said Angela, jumping up yet again. "But when we were in Miss Spender's class, Miss Spender said . . ."

Miss Bennett slammed the jar of tadpoles down on my desk with such a crash that some of the water slopped over the top. I watched the tadpoles wriggling with fright and I knew just how they felt.

"Angela Mitchell!" snapped Miss Bennett. "I don't want to hear one more word from you today. You will please stand outside the door for the remainder of the lesson. And when you go home you will write out fifty times, 'I must not speak until I'm spoken to' and bring it to me on Monday morning."

I could tell by Angela's face that she was furious. Her mouth went all sulky and she stalked out of the room. I even thought she was going to slam the door, but there are some things that even Angela daren't do. She was still furious when school finished for the day and we started walking home together.

"That Miss Bennett is an old cat," she muttered, with a scowl. "I'm never going to speak to her again. Not ever!"

"Oh, Angela," I said. "You don't really mean that." Angela stamped her foot in temper and pushed me away from her.

"You're pathetic," she said. "I most certainly do mean it. And if you were a proper sort of friend, YOU wouldn't speak to her again EITHER!"

We went home and I didn't see Angela at all on Saturday or Sunday because my mum and dad and I drove up to Newcastle that night to stay with my grandma, and she's my dad's mother and she's kind and fat and cuddly and she bakes the best stottie cakes in the North East. We didn't get back until very late on Sunday evening, so the next time I saw Angela was on Monday morning. And that was when she came round and told me she'd lost her voice.

Well, can you blame me if I didn't believe her? I looked at her suspiciously, and she had that sparkly look in her eyes that always means she's up to something.

"You haven't really lost your voice," I said. "Not really and truly. It's a trick. It's just so you won't have to talk to Miss Bennett, isn't it?" But she shook her head and pointed into her mouth.

"Laryngitis," she whispered, and gave a husky sort of giggle, and I started to giggle too. I thought it was the funniest joke she had ever thought of, and I couldn't wait to see what happened when she tried it out on Miss Bennett.

So off we went to school and the first thing Miss Bennett said when we went into the classroom after prayers was "Well, Angela? Did you do your lines?"

Angela smiled politely and nodded her head. She opened her satchel and put some sheets of paper on Miss Bennett's desk.

"Thank you, Angela," said Miss Bennett. "I hope this has taught you a lesson. We'll say no more about it, but I would like you to promise that it won't happen again."

Angela opened and shut her mouth once or twice and made a funny little croaking sound. I had to stuff my hanky in my mouth to stop myself from laughing when she solemnly shook her head and pointed her finger down her throat.

"Can't . . ." she whispered, "Can't talk."

"Oh, dear," said Miss Bennett. "What's the matter, Angela? Have you lost your voice or something?" Angela nodded hard and Miss Bennett gave her a sympathetic little smile.

"Well, I'm sorry to hear that," she said. "But at least it means we'll all get some peace and quiet for a couple of days." Everybody laughed when Miss Bennett said that, because it was a joke, and you always have to laugh at teachers' jokes. Angela went to her seat, blushing and scowling, and I heard Laurence Parker hiss "Dummy!" at her as she went past.

"And now let's get on with our poetry lesson," said Miss Bennett. "We've wasted enough time this morning. I hope you've all learnt your poem over the weekend. Charlotte, will you please stand up and recite the first few lines of Wordsworth's 'Daffodils'."

I got up and took a quick peep over my shoulder at Angela. And then I suddenly went cold all over because she was staring at me in a funny sort of way and telling me something with her eyes. I knew what she wanted me to do. She wanted me to prove that I was a proper sort of friend. She wanted me to pretend that I'd lost my voice too, so that I wouldn't have to speak to Miss Bennett either.

"Well, come along, Charlotte," said Miss Bennett impatiently. "You haven't forgotten it, surely?"

I gazed miserably down at my desk and thought if Angela was brave enough to do it then I must be too, or she would never forgive me. She would choose somebody else to be her best friend and it would probably be that awful Delilah Jones. I opened my mouth.

"I wandered lonely . . ." I whispered, and then stopped. Miss Bennett stared at me suspiciously.

"What's the matter?" she said in a stern voice.

I pointed down my throat and shook my head, just as Angela had done. Miss Bennett looked from me to Angela and then back again.

"Charlotte Ellis!" she said sharply. "This is quite ridiculous! You can't mean that you've lost your voice, too?" I nodded dumbly and Miss Bennett's face went pink and some of the boys started to snigger.

"I'm afraid I find this very hard to believe," said Miss Bennett icily. "That you should both happen to lose your voices on the same day. I don't suppose either of you has a note from your doctor?"

I shook my head again and looked at Angela, expecting her to do the same. Now we're for it, I thought. But Angela was rummaging in her satchel and then I couldn't believe my eyes because she got out a small white envelope and took it to Miss Bennett with a polite smile. My heart sank into a big, heavy lump at the bottom of my stomach.

Miss Bennett opened the envelope and read the note.

"This is indeed from Angela's doctor," she said. "It explains that Angela has a mild throat ailment and has lost her voice. It says that it is not serious or infectious, however, and she is quite well enough to attend school providing she stays indoors at break times." Miss Bennett folded the note and glared at me over the top of her glasses.

"Well, Charlotte? I suppose you have a note from your doctor?"

I swallowed and croaked weakly, "No, Miss Bennett."

"And in fact you haven't lost your voice at all," said Miss Bennett in an ominous sort of way.

I hung my head. "No, Miss Bennett," I said.

"Then what is your explanation for this strange behaviour?"

"It was . . . it was a joke," I mumbled. Everybody tittered and giggled and Miss Bennett looked round the room with a stern expression.

"I'm afraid none of us find that sort of joke in the least amusing, do we?" she said to the class. And they all stopped sniggering and shook their heads solemnly, and doesn't it make you sick the way everybody always agrees with the teacher?

"Charlotte, you will stay indoors at break time and clean out the art cupboard as a punishment," said Miss Bennett. "And you will please try to behave more sensibly in future."

"Yes, Miss Bennett. Thank you, Miss Bennett," I breathed gratefully. Cleaning out the art cupboard is a horrible, mucky job and it makes your hands all filthy, but it's a lot better than some of the punishments Miss Bennett manages to think up. So I felt I was quite lucky really and I didn't mind too much when everybody else trooped out to play at the end of the lesson. Anyway, it meant that I could stay indoors with Angela, and do you know, she didn't laugh a bit about me making such a right idiot of myself about the laryngitis, and she even started to help me tidy the cupboard. But that was when the other awful thing happened.

I was clearing out all the junk which had been shoved to the back of the cupboard when I came across an old, battered tin. I heaved it out and looked at the label and it said Cow Gum. I laughed and showed it to Angela.

"I wonder if that's for sticking cows," I said. Then I started to put it away again on one of the shelves but Angela leaned over and took it out of my hands. Her face had sort of lighted up and I could see that she'd had one of her wicked ideas.

"What are you doing?" I said anxiously. Angela found a stick and prised off the lid of the tin and we both looked inside. A thick layer of glue lay at the bottom, all sticky and shiny like varnish. Angela gazed at it for a minute, then she skipped away across the room with the tin in her hands. She stopped beside Miss Bennett's chair and started to dip the stick in the glue. I gave a shriek of horror.

"Angela! Don't!" I pleaded. "Not Miss Bennett's chair!"

Angela turned and waved the stick at me. "You're right," she whispered hoarsely. "I think I'll use it on a pig, instead." She crossed the room quickly, and before I could even try to stop her she had scraped out a big dollop of glue and spread it all over the seat of Laurence Parker's chair.

She pushed the tin of glue back in the cupboard just in time because that moment the bell rang for the end of break and the other children started to come back into the classroom. That nosy Delilah Jones began to wrinkle her face and sniff as soon as she came into the room.

"What's that funny smell?" she asked. But Angela only shrugged her shoulders and looked blank, and I turned my back and went on putting all the stuff back in the cupboard. I didn't know what else to do.

When I had finished I went back to my place and sat down. I had a quick peep at Laurence Parker's chair and you couldn't tell there was glue on it at all. It only looked a bit more shiny than usual. Then I saw Laurence Parker come into the room so I put my head inside my desk because I just couldn't bear to watch him sit down.

I knew Miss Bennett had come in because all the chattering suddenly stopped and I heard everybody scuttling to their places.

"We're going to do some spelling now," came Miss Bennett's voice. "Take out your green spelling books, please, everybody. You may have five minutes to revise the twenty words we did last week, and then I'll test you on them."

I grabbed my spelling book and when I put down my desk lid I saw that Laurence Parker was sitting in his place next to me and he hadn't noticed a thing. I looked over my shoulder, but Angela had her head down over her book and didn't look up.

It was all quiet for a few minutes while everybody except me practised their words and then Miss Bennett stood up.

"We'll start with the front row," she said. "I'll ask each of you to spell one word for me. Now, Delilah. You're first. Your word is, enough."

And that awful Delilah Jones leaped up, looking all smug and pleased with herself. "E N O U G H," she said, and Miss Bennett smiled at her and said, "Well done," and you should have seen Delilah Jones smirking all over her silly face.

Well, it went all the way along the front row and then all the way along the next row and then it was our row and I started to get that horrible feeling in my stomach that's called butterflies and I don't know why it's called getting butterflies because I think it feels more like great big creepy crawly caterpillars. And it was my turn at last and Miss Bennett said "Pneumonia, Charlotte," and it was the hardest word on the list and I should have known Miss Bennett would save that one for me. Of course I knew how to spell it. But how could I think straight? How could anybody think straight if they knew that it was Laurence Parker's turn next and he was sitting there glued to his seat?

I stood up quickly. "New what?" I said stupidly, and Miss Bennett's mouth went all squeezed up at the corners as if she was sucking a lemon.

"Pneumonia," she said again.

"Um, er, N E W ..." I began and Laurence Parker gave a snigger.

"Sit down, Charlotte," said Miss Bennett crossly. "It's obvious you don't know it. You must write it out three times in your book and learn it for next week. Perhaps Laurence Parker can do better. Laurence? Pneumonia, please."

There was a sort of horrible clatter as Laurence Parker got to his feet and I didn't know where to look because of course his chair was stuck firmly to the seat of his trousers and had got up with him. His face went all red and he swung around to try to see what was the matter, but that only made things worse because the legs of the chair crashed into the desk behind. Miss Bennett's face went as black as thunder and everybody stared like anything and there were a few smothered giggles, but nobody dared laugh out loud.

"What on earth are you doing, boy?" snapped Miss Bennett and Laurence Parker started twisting about and trying to pull himself free, but the chair was well and truly stuck.

"Laurence Parker! Come here AT ONCE!" shouted Miss Bennett. "I will not tolerate this sort of clowning during my lessons!"

Laurence Parker hunched his shoulders and shuffled forward to the front of the class, clutching the chair to his bottom with his hands. He looked a bit like a fat, old tortoise with its house on its back.

"I . . . I seem to have got stuck," he stammered miserably, and Miss Bennett clucked and tutted and fussed. Then she put one hand on his shoulder and the other on the back of the chair and pulled.

There was a dreadful ripping noise and there stood Miss Bennett looking a bit surprised with the chair in her hand and hanging from the chair was a big piece of grey material. And there stood Laurence Parker looking even more surprised with a great big ragged hole in the seat of his trousers and you could see his blue and red striped Marks and Spencers underwear. Everybody stared in horror and the whole room went dead quiet and all you could hear was people breathing and that was when I started to laugh.

It wouldn't have been so bad if it had been a quiet little giggle, or a subdued sort of chuckle, but it wasn't. It was a horrible loud cackle. My dad says that when I laugh I sound like an old hen laying an egg. And I always seem to laugh at the wrong time and in the wrong place and sometimes it gets me into terrible trouble, but I can't help it. Like the time at the vicar's garden party when Miss Menzies sneezed and her false teeth flew out and landed in the bowl of fruit punch. And that other time when we went to my Auntie Fiona's wedding up in Gateshead and my grandad trod on the end of the bride's long white veil as she was walking down the aisle and yanked it clean off her head and I laughed so much that I was sent out of the church and had to wait outside in the car so I missed the whole thing.

Anyway, Laurence Parker looked so funny standing there with that great hole in his trousers that if I hadn't laughed I'd have burst. My eyes streamed with tears and this time it was no use stuffing my hanky in my mouth because it only made me choke and laugh even more. And then of course when I started laughing like that it set everybody else off as well and soon the whole class was laughing like anything and you should have heard the din.

Miss Bennett started to thump on her desk with her fist and I knew I was in bad trouble because she only does that when she's really mad. And when I saw the way she was glaring at me I wished I hadn't laughed so much because, of course, that was what made her think it was me who had been messing about with the rotten old glue.

"There is glue on this chair," said Miss Bennett, sort of quietly and ominously. "And I don't have to ask who is responsible for this outrage." Her eyes bored into me and I felt my face go scarlet. "There were only two people left in this room at break time, and one of them has guilt written all over her face." Miss Bennett turned to Laurence Parker, who had backed up against the wall to hide his underwear and was standing there looking daggers at me.

"Laurence," she said, quite gently. "You had better go and wait in the boys' changing room. I'm going to phone your mother and ask her to bring you a spare pair of trousers." Then she turned back to me and her voice would have frozen the Sahara Desert. "Charlotte Ellis, you will stay behind after school this afternoon. You and I must have a very serious talk."

Well, of course I sort of hoped that Angela would stand up and confess, but I must admit I wasn't all that surprised when she didn't because I know what she's like. And I didn't get a single chance to speak to her on her own for the rest of that day, as she had to stay indoors again at lunchtime because of her sore throat. So when four o'clock came, everybody went home and I had to stay behind and get told off, and it was awful because Miss Bennett went on and on at me until I thought she'd never stop and all I could do was stand there and say nothing because of course she knew that it could only have been me or Angela and I couldn't tell on my friend, could I? Even if she did deserve it.

When at last she let me go and I escaped out of the school door, who should be waiting for me at the gate but Angela, and she had waited for me in the cold all that time. But when she squeezed my arm and whispered that I was the best friend in the whole world I pressed my lips tight together and walked away from her, because this time she'd gone too far and at least she could have taken a bit of the blame.

And then when I got home I suddenly felt a whole lot better, because my dad was there. And I told him all about it because I always tell my dad everything, and he said I was quite right not to tell on my friend.

But he said Angela was a right little minx and it was high time I gave her the push and found myself a new best friend who wouldn't keep getting me into trouble.

I thought about that, and in the end I made up my mind that he was right. I even managed not to speak to Angela for three whole days.

But somehow life is never so much fun without her, and when she came round on the third day, looking as sorry as can be and carrying her favourite picture of Elton John as a peace offering, I couldn't help feeling glad to see her and I hadn't the heart to stay cross with her any longer.

Written by Sheila Lavelle,
illustrated by Alice Englander

Rules for coping with bullies

1 Don't live in the same street as one.

BULLY ST.
VICTORIA AVENUE
SUNNY CRESCENT

2 Make friends with someone large.

3 If possible, stay cool. Bullies find this boring and will soon get tired of teasing you.

4 Keep out of their way. They usually pick on the nearest person.

...Uh? Where did he go?

38

5

Make them laugh.
This could be hard, as
bullies aren't famous for
their sense of humour.

6

Most bullies are not
very bright. Try and
outwit them.

Try being friendly.
They're not used to this
and might faint from
shock.

7

8

Best of all, stand up
to them. Bullies are also
cowards.

A Fuss over Eggs

Aldo Sossi is a vegetarian, and his first lunch hour at his new school is a disaster when his jar of apple sauce is broken. Immediately Aldo is nicknamed Applesauce, a name he hates. Only DeDe acts friendly, but she's a bit weird. After all, who ever heard of a girl wearing a fake moustache in school? Trying to stay out of trouble, Aldo decides never to take apple sauce in his lunch again, but on Monday . . .

He did have an egg.

When Aldo took the items out of his lunch box on Monday, DeDe watched him carefully. He placed the hard-boiled egg on the table and reached for the cheese sandwich that was also in his box.

"No peanut butter today?" she asked. She was chewing away on a chopped liver sandwich. It was on a big roll and it looked good, if you liked chopped liver.

Aldo moved his chair a couple of inches away from her so he wouldn't have to smell her sandwich. "No peanut butter," he said, biting into his cheese.

"Hey, Applesauce, where's your sauce?" asked a boy at the next table. He wasn't even in Aldo's class, but the name had spread. In the morning when he arrived at school, a couple of boys had greeted him with the name. Aldo hoped the habit would wear off with time.

"Tell me about your dog," he asked DeDe, to change the subject.

"Well," said DeDe, removing her moustache, "I've had her for a year. And I'm teaching her tricks. I'm teaching her to cross only at green lights and not at red." "I'm not sure," said Aldo, "but I think I read somewhere that dogs are colour blind." "Not Cookie," DeDe insisted.

Just then an arm reached between Aldo and DeDe and grabbed Aldo's egg. The arm tossed it to another boy. He tossed it to another, and the egg started making the rounds of the lunchroom. Aldo watched in amazement, wondering when the dinner ladies would stop the game.

"Whose egg is this?" one of the dinner ladies demanded. "Food is not to be played with, only eaten." She was a big woman and looked as if she ate lots of eggs and meat, and cakes and ice cream, too.

Aldo did not want to admit that the egg was his. Next they would be calling him Eggnog, he thought.

"Where did you get this egg?" the dinner lady asked the last boy who had caught it. He grinned and pointed to the fellow who had thrown it to him.

"And where did you get it?" she asked him. Obviously she wanted to track the egg back to its source. When she gets to me, I'll tell her I got it from a chicken, thought Aldo. But when the dinner lady did reach him, he was too embarrassed. "It was in my lunch," was all he said.

"Then eat it!" she said, handing the egg to Aldo.

The shell was cracked and dirty from all the grubby hands that had held it since he had taken it out of his lunch box. Aldo didn't say anything, but he knew he wasn't going to be able to eat the egg. And he didn't think he would be able to bring another one in his lunch ever again, either. What would his mother say about that!

"You think you're so funny!" said DeDe, turning to the boy who had first grabbed Aldo's egg. "Someday you'll get in big trouble."

"Oh, yeah? Who with—you?"

"Maybe," said DeDe, shrugging her shoulders and turning back to Aldo.

"You think you're so funny!" And DeDe suddenly poked Aldo. Her moustache was back in place, but underneath it he could see her lips twitching into a smile. "Bring another egg tomorrow," she whispered.

"No," said Aldo.

"You must," she pleaded. "I've got a plan."

"Then you bring one, if you want it," said Aldo.

"You must," DeDe whispered urgently.

Aldo turned in his chair and pretended to be absorbed in the textbook in front of him. Why should he bring another hard-boiled egg to school and risk getting into trouble with it?

When school was over for the day, DeDe followed Aldo outside. "I have a great idea," she said, "but you must bring an egg tomorrow for it to work."

"Why don't *you* bring an egg?" said Aldo. "Why should I be the one?"

"I hate eggs. I haven't eaten one since I was a baby, so my mother would never cook one for me. But you could bring one without any problem."

"It's no problem for *you* if I bring an egg, just me," said Aldo. The thought crossed Aldo's mind that DeDe was the one who was responsible for knocking his container of apple sauce onto the floor last week. If not for her, he wouldn't have got stuck with that stupid nickname. Now she was hatching a new scheme to mortify him with eggs.

"Trust me," said DeDe. "Aren't I your friend?"

Aldo looked at DeDe. He knew she hadn't meant to knock the apple sauce down. It was an accident. He was glad that DeDe considered herself to be his friend.

"OK," he agreed. "I'll bring an egg tomorrow."
Yet afterward, walking home toward Hillside Lane,
Aldo felt he had consented too quickly. He should
have said that he would bring an egg to school
only on condition that she explain why she wore
her silly moustache. Aldo was beginning to get
used to it like the other kids in the class. But still
he was curious about why she wore it.

At lunchtime the next day, DeDe reached eagerly for
the egg that was in Aldo's lunch box next to his
cream-cheese-and-jam sandwich. She placed
it conspicuously between
them on the table.

47

"What's the matter with you?" asked Aldo. "Do you want someone to grab it again?"

"Yes!" DeDe grinned.

Sure enough, the boy at the next table again made a grab for the egg and threw it to one of his friends. The egg passed through at least half a dozen hands before the dinner lady was able to stop them. This time she walked straight to where Aldo was sitting. "Is this your egg?" she asked, holding up the dirty, cracked oval.

"Yes, but I didn't throw it," said Aldo.

"Well, it certainly didn't fly across the room," she said.

Somebody spilled something at another table, making a commotion and distracting her attention. Aldo turned to DeDe.

"See. I told you I would get into trouble."

"Don't worry," whispered DeDe. "I have a plan."

"Some plan," grumbled Aldo. "I don't want to be involved in your dumb plan."

She didn't say anything more. Even during the afternoon, when they were working in committees on an art project and she could easily have spoken, DeDe said nothing. But when school ended, she followed closely behind Aldo.

"Bring another egg tomorrow," she said softly under her moustache.

"Never!" said Aldo.

"You must!" said DeDe.

"That's what you said yesterday," said Aldo, turning away from her. "Some friend you are!" Then he turned and ran off toward home.

Aldo worried about his mother giving him an egg in his lunch the next day, but he needn't have. She was not likely to give him eggs three days in a row. Even though she worried about his eating enough protein, she also worried about his eating too much cholesterol, which was something that was in eggs. So when Aldo sat down at the lunch table, he had only a peanut-butter sandwich and a carrot in his lunch box.

Aldo had not wanted to sit next to DeDe today, but there was no other vacant seat. He bit into his carrot and didn't say anything as she removed her food from her box.

To Aldo's surprise, she removed an egg, which was wrapped in a napkin, and placed it on the table between them.

"I thought you didn't like eggs," said Aldo.

"I don't," said DeDe, removing her moustache and biting into a sardine sandwich.

"Then why did you bring it?" Aldo started to ask.

But before he had finished his question, a hand reached between them and grabbed the egg and threw it across the room. Aldo watched as another boy held out his hand to make the catch. The egg smashed in his hand, oozing all over his shirt sleeve. It was raw!

Aldo looked at DeDe. She was calmly chewing on her sandwich as if nothing had happened. All around them children were shouting and laughing, but DeDe was acting as if raw eggs flew through the air every day.

The dinner lady marched over to Aldo.

"Was that your idea of a joke?" she asked.

"No," said Aldo honestly. He was about to say that he hadn't even brought the egg to school, but he didn't want to tell on DeDe.

"I don't play with food," he said.

"I don't think anyone else will after this either," said the dinner lady. For the first time she smiled at Aldo. "That was a good trick. He deserved it," she said, as she walked off.

Aldo looked at DeDe. She was putting her moustache back on as she always did after lunch. Even though it hid most of her mouth, he could see that she was smiling at him.

"I told you I couldn't bring a hard-boiled egg," she said. "So I brought a raw one."

Johanna Hurwitz,
illustrated by *Maria Yeap*

CRACK A YOLK!

WHERE DO WE GET IT?

PEANUT BUTTER

Underground? And I thought peanuts grew on trees!

We peanuts are peculiar plants The way we push each pod And peg it down and hold it safe Beneath the warm red clod.

1 October to December: Peanuts are planted.

2 They grow into small bushy plants up to 50 cm high. Little yellow peanut-shaped flowers appear. Their stalks (or pegs, as the peanut-farmers call them) get longer and longer and bend towards the ground. The young pods at the end of the pegs are pushed right into the ground.

3 March to May: the peanut plants are lifted by machines and laid in the sun to dry, or they are dried in special drying bins.

4 About two weeks later they are threshed — a machine separates the nuts from the plants.

5 Cleaned peanuts are sent in bags to peanut-butter factories, where they are shelled and crushed.

This Kingaroy sun is just the thing to bring out my full flavour.

There are about 500 peanut kernels in a 375 gram jar of peanut butter.

And peanuts first came from South America.

Start at the bottom and read your way up the page and back again...

Pure PEANUT BUTTER

55

Eggs-actly so

The biggest egg hunt was in Georgia, USA, on 7th April 1985. 72,000 hard-boiled eggs and 40,000 sweet eggs were hidden.

Shell-shocked !

Two blind people who worked in a kitchen shelled 12,600 hard-boiled eggs in a 7¼-hour shift on 23rd April 1971 in Trowbridge, Wiltshire.

The largest omelette in the world was made from 45,000 eggs in a pan measuring 3.05 metres by 13.11 metres. It was cooked in Vancouver, Canada, on 27th January 1986.

The greatest number of two-egg omelettes made in 30 minutes is 315. They were made at a restaurant in Providence, Rhode Island, USA, on 29th June 1985.

Egg Faces

Every circus clown has his own style of make-up. No two clowns can look exactly the same. A new clown must have his make-up design recorded on an egg shell so that it cannot be copied.

57

Eggs-ercise!

Chris Riggio of San Francisco, USA, ran a
28.5 mile (45.86 kilometres) course carrying
an egg on a dessert spoon. It took him
4 hours and 34 minutes, and he did this on
7th October 1979.

In Finland on 6th September 1982, Risto
Antikainen threw a fresh hen's egg to Jyrki
Korhonen over a distance of 96.9 metres.
The egg didn't break!

He has eaten:
14 hard-boiled eggs in 58 seconds (February 1977)

13 raw eggs in 1 second (May 1984)

38 soft-boiled eggs in 75 seconds (May 1984).

Easter Eggs
Easter Eggs

The traditional game of pace-egging takes place in Preston, Lancashire, on Easter Monday. Children roll eggs down the slopes of Avenham Park to the River Ribble.

Wow! The tallest egg in the world!

It's enormous!

It's amazing!

Cor!

Wow!

The tallest Easter egg in the world was exhibited by the Patisserie Eueen Lauwers, Belgium, in March 1983. It measured 5.42 metres, and weighed 2323 kilograms.

The sport of egg-tapping is still popular. An egg is held firmly by a player, who then taps it against his opponent's egg, hoping to break it.

Your weight is 3430 kilograms.

Made at Macopa Patisserie, Leicester, England, 7th April 1982.

An American custom at Easter is to paint hard-boiled eggs, which are then tied to a tree or bush in the garden.

61

Fabergé Eggs

Peter Carl Fabergé, goldsmith and court jeweller to the Tsars of Russia in the nineteenth century, designed many jewelled eggs as magnificent presents for the European Royal Families. Each egg was different and contained a surprise gift. Most of the eggs are so expensive that ordinary people today cannot afford them, and they are in the collections of kings and queens around the world.

A nest of eggs

Glossary

absorbed (*p. 46*)
so interested that you forget everything around you

brasso (*p. 12*)
a special polish for brass

cholesterol (*p. 50*)
a white substance found in eggs and other food

albatross (*p. 17*)
large white seabird

coleslaw (*p. 6*)
a salad made from carrots and white cabbage

commotion (*p. 49*)
a lot of noise

consented (*p. 47*)
agreed

clod (*p. 55*)
a lump of clay or earth

conspicuously (*p. 47*)
easily seen

contented (*p. 8*)
happy; satisfied

eggnog (*p. 43*)
a drink made from eggs, milk, sugar and spices

flustered (*p. 19*)
upset and confused

distracting (*p. 49*)
to make a person lose their concentration

gleaming (*p. 4*)
shining

inclined to be vague (*p. 5*)
absent-minded; often forget things

indignant (*p. 11*)
angry

hoarse (*p. 19*)
when the voice is rough and croaky

infectious (*p. 26*)
can be caught by another person

mortify (*p. 46*)
embarrass; make someone feel ashamed

kneaded (*p. 8*)
pressed

minx (*p. 37*)
cheeky girl

muffle (*p. 7*)
make quieter

ominously (*p. 35*)
as if something terrible is going to happen soon

opponent (*p. 61*)
person you play against in a game

63

Glossary continues on page 64

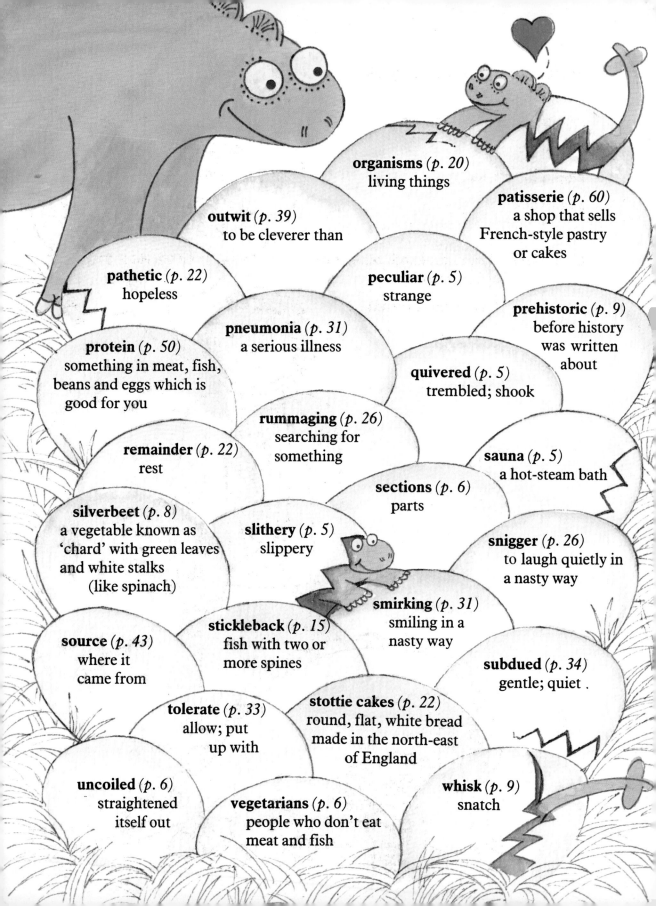

organisms (*p. 20*)
living things

patisserie (*p. 60*)
a shop that sells
French-style pastry
or cakes

outwit (*p. 39*)
to be cleverer than

peculiar (*p. 5*)
strange

pathetic (*p. 22*)
hopeless

prehistoric (*p. 9*)
before history
was written
about

pneumonia (*p. 31*)
a serious illness

protein (*p. 50*)
something in meat, fish,
beans and eggs which is
good for you

quivered (*p. 5*)
trembled; shook

rummaging (*p. 26*)
searching for
something

remainder (*p. 22*)
rest

sauna (*p. 5*)
a hot-steam bath

sections (*p. 6*)
parts

silverbeet (*p. 8*)
a vegetable known as
'chard' with green leaves
and white stalks
(like spinach)

slithery (*p. 5*)
slippery

snigger (*p. 26*)
to laugh quietly in
a nasty way

smirking (*p. 31*)
smiling in a
nasty way

source (*p. 43*)
where it
came from

stickleback (*p. 15*)
fish with two or
more spines

subdued (*p. 34*)
gentle; quiet .

tolerate (*p. 33*)
allow; put
up with

stottie cakes (*p. 22*)
round, flat, white bread
made in the north-east
of England

uncoiled (*p. 6*)
straightened
itself out

vegetarians (*p. 6*)
people who don't eat
meat and fish

whisk (*p. 9*)
snatch